13 February to 5 June 2016
The Holburne Museum, Bath

Impressionism
Capturing Life

Jennifer Scott

Acknowledgements

The Holburne has a particular strength in British 18th-century portraiture, with major works by, among others, Thomas Gainsborough, Joshua Reynolds, Johan Zoffany and Allan Ramsay. This exhibition, which takes place in the year that we celebrate one hundred years in our current building, also marks the fact that the first Impressionist exhibition of 1874 was held in the year of the death of our founder, Sir William Holburne.

I am grateful to the Holburne Museum team for their support in all areas of preparing for this exhibition, especially to Howard Batho. It was my predecessor, Alexander Sturgis, who first conceived the show, negotiated many of the loans and graciously encouraged me to bring it to completion. My heartfelt thanks also to Christopher Lloyd and MaryAnne Stevens for sharing their profound expertise and to Professor Stephen Farthing, whose rich commentary on the exhibition audio guide aptly brings the exhibition's theme to life.

I am immensely grateful to the lenders to this exhibition. These paintings are jewels in the crown of their respective collections, and it is an honour to have them on our walls in Bath. In particular I would like to thank Andrew Brownsword, Nicholas Burrows, Aisha Burtenshaw, Nicola Kalinsky, Vicky Skelding-Bloor, Joan Lyall, Philip Wise, Pippa Stephenson, Duncan Dornan, Karen Stewart, Fiona McKellar, Maria Balshaw, Siân Millar, Michael Clarke, Janice Slater, Greta Casacci, Nicholas Penny, Gabriele Finaldi, Caroline Campbell, Sarah Hardy, Samantha Saward, Andrea Kusel, Michael Durning, Richard Green, Rachel Boyd Hall, Tim Craven, Rebecca Moisan, Alice Calloway, Caroline Collier, Sanne Klinge, Stephen Snoddy and Julie Brown.

Finally, I would like to thank the Principal Sponsor of this exhibition, Bath Spa University. Already our cultural partners, this additional support is hugely appreciated and highly appropriate. The reputation of the Bath School of Art and Design at the University represents the approach to artistic practice and theory advocated by the artists in this exhibition: 'pioneers of the painting of the future', lighting up the creative world.

Jennifer Scott *Director*
Holburne Museum

'Real and Existing Things':
Impressionism in Context

We see an interior of a house, light streaming through from a nearby door. A woman sits with her hands resting on her lap, caught in her own thoughts. The artist has depicted her with the detachment afforded to an inanimate object in a still-life painting. The bustle of the everyday world seemingly continues beyond the room, but this portrait captures a soundless moment, isolated from the confines of time and place.

This could be an account of a painting by the Dutch Masters Pieter de Hooch or Jan Vermeer, celebrated for their popular 17th-century depictions of private moments. Instead it describes a painting by Camille Pissarro, self-consciously quoting from Dutch art of the past but which, when it was created in 1896, was both relevant and poignant. Comparison of Pissarro's *Petite Bonne Flamande dite 'La Rosa'* (Little Flemish Maid, called 'La Rosa') (cat 5) with Pieter de Hooch's *The Courtyard of a House in Delft*, 1658 (National Gallery, London) (fig 1) indicates that Pissarro employed the same motifs to create spaces within spaces, with doorways leading into distinct areas. De Hooch's woman standing in the corridor seemingly awaits the arrival of another person, but something about the turn of her body and the position of her head, even from behind, alerts us to her self-absorption. This is intensified by the action of mother and child in a separate zone on the right, caught in conversation and movement. The steep angle of the stone floor in the 17th-century painting and the parquet floor in Pissarro's scene – and the broom in the former and the chair in the latter – form visual barriers to our view, thereby separating the painted world from that of reality.

Pissarro was an influential figure in the development of Impressionism, arguably the most increasingly popular visual arts movement of all time. However, in the 19th century these artists were outsiders, working against the established centre of the French art world, the Académie des Beaux-Arts in Paris, which had rejected them for inclusion in their eminent annual exhibition (the Salon).

In April 1874 the first Impressionist exhibition was held in Paris, featuring works by, among others, Claude Monet, Paul Cézanne, Edgar Degas, Berthe Morisot, Camille Pissarro, Pierre-Auguste Renoir and Alfred Sisley. The group went by the somewhat unwieldy name of the 'Limited Corporation of Artists, Painters, Sculptors, Engravers and Lithographers'. Their first joint aim was

cat 5

Camille Pissarro (1830–1903)
Petite bonne flamande dite 'La Rosa',
1896
Oil on canvas
54.6 x 45.1 cm

Richard Green Gallery, London

fig 1

Pieter de Hooch (1629–1684)
The Courtyard of a House in Delft,
1658
Oil on canvas
73.5 x 60.0 cm

National Gallery, London
NG 835

to stage an alternative rival exhibition to open two weeks before the official Paris Salon. The title 'Impressionist' was coined by Louis Leroy in a satirical review of this exhibition for *Le Charivari*.

The appellation was taken up by the journalist Jules-Antoine Castagnary who wrote 'We will have to invent the new term "impressionists". They… render not the landscape itself but the sensation produced by the landscape'. It is probably due to this influential definition that Impressionism is often thought of as a landscape-dominated art form. But as this exhibition at the Holburne Museum aims to demonstrate, all the leading Impressionist artists, with the notable exception of Sisley, focused on the interaction of the human figure with the world.

The Impressionist artists were united through their rejection from the establishment, but each had distinguishing artistic approaches. Their new style of painting grew out of the trend for naturalism, practised in the mid-19th century particularly by Gustave Courbet (1819–1877). Courbet's *Realist Manifesto* of 1855 described a scientific description of the observed world. He expanded on this in 1861 when he wrote of painting as 'essentially a concrete art' which 'does not consist of anything but the representation of real and existing things'.

The ability to capture the fleeting essence of a moment typifies the Impressionist approach. The results were not wholeheartedly denigrated, despite the enduring notion that the Impressionists were unrecognised geniuses in their own time. As Paul Tucker remarked in an article in 1986 '…we have generally overlooked the fact that while a few critics gave the [first Impressionist] exhibition scathing reviews, more liked it than not'. Of fourteen reviews, six were very positive, three were mixed, and only five were negative. The Impressionist artists reacted against the limitations of the art establishment in order to create, in the words of their contemporary, the critic Arsène Alexandre, 'bold cutting-edge works', which resonated throughout Europe and beyond.

'The Painting of the Future'

A Review in *La Presse* of the First Impressionist exhibition described the 'nauseating and revolting' 'debaucheries' of this type of painting, and yet acknowledged that the artists were offering 'not just an alternative to the Salon, but a new road… for those who think art, in order to develop, needs more freedom than that granted by the administration'. The artists were hailed as 'pioneers of the painting of the future'. Painting outdoors ('en plein air'), focusing on shifting light and form, using divided brushwork, and creating series of images of the same view at varying times of day in order to convey a sense of the transience of nature, are just some of the innovations that characterise the Impressionist approach. This was eloquently expressed by the self-taught artist Paul Signac (1863–1935):

> *'In the matter of technique, these painters are innovators; by a more logical and scientific arrangement of tones and colours they are replacing outdated procedures…… In moral terms, the example they set for our sensual generation is all too rare: faithful to their idea of art, convinced of the superiority of their methods, they remain poor at a time when they might, as so many others have done, at the cost of a few compromises enjoy the favour of the standard, influential critics, whose stale prose translates for the artist into gold, honours and decorations.*

> *……the impressionist artists, expelled from the community of art like revolutionaries from society, would deserve a sympathetic greeting from those who applaud the breakdown of all prejudice and all routine.*

> *[They are]…revolutionaries by temperament, who, departing from the beaten track, paint what they see, as they feel it, and, often unconsciously, give a solid pick blow to the old social edifice, which, worm-eaten, cracks and crumbles like some abandoned cathedral.'*

Paul Signac, 'Impressionists and Revolutionaries', *La Révolte*, 1891

cat 1

John Singer Sargent (1856–1925)
*Claude Monet Painting by
the Edge of a Wood*, 1885
Oil on canvas
54.0 x 64.8 cm

Tate N04103
Presented by Miss Emily
Sargent and Mrs Ormond through
the Art Fund, 1925

Claude Monet (1840–1926) is often hailed as the father of Impressionism, after his landscape *Impression: Sunrise* was included in the first Impressionist exhibition of 1874. This portrait by the American artist Singer Sargent captures Monet at work while his wife sits nearby. The two artists were friends and had painted together at Giverny in 1885, the year of this portrait. Sargent was an enthusiastic practitioner of the loose handling and informal approach of Impressionism, particularly evidenced here in the featureless faces of the sitters.

Although drawing outdoors had been a standard practice of landscape artists from the 17th century onwards, painting 'en plein air' directly onto canvas was a typically Impressionist innovation. Monet painted scenes on the spot in order to capture the true effects of light and colour, and sometimes even practical details from the scene such as, in his Normandy beach scenes, grains of sand embedded in the paint layer. The result makes the viewer feel that they can smell the atmosphere itself, and feel the sensation of fresh air transported through the finished picture. Such informality became synonymous with the Impressionists' work, even though the majority of the artists worked more traditionally in studios.

cat 2

Mary Cassatt (1844–1926)
The Young Girls, 1885
Oil on canvas
46.3 x 55.5 cm

Glasgow Life (Glasgow Museums)
on behalf of Glasgow City Council
Acc No 2980
Presented by the Trustees of the
Hamilton Bequest, 1953

Cassatt first exhibited with the Impressionists in 1879. The daughter of a Pittsburgh businessman, she trained in Philadelphia before travelling to Europe and settling in Paris. The economy of finish in this depiction of two girls is typical of Cassatt's spontaneous style which belies her careful construction and draughtsmanship (she shared her belief in the importance of drawing with her friend Edgar Degas, see cat 3). The bond between the two girls, probably sisters, is demonstrated by the closeness of their cheeks and the familiarity of their embrace. The striking green background evokes an outdoor setting, as though the girls are sitting on a grassy bank. The simplicity of form has led to the supposition that this is an unfinished work, particularly because the girls' dresses are only roughly blocked out, but the fact that it is signed probably indicates the contrary.

Edgar Degas (1834–1917)
Hélène Rouart in her Father's Study,
c. 1886
Oil on canvas
162.5 x 121 cm

National Gallery, London
NG6469

Unlike Claude Monet (see cat 1), Degas did not paint 'en plein air',
but he was equally important in the foundation of the Impressionist
movement and participated in, and helped to organise, all but one
of the eight Impressionist exhibitions. The son of wealthy parents,
he was taught in Paris by a pupil of Jean-Auguste-Dominique Ingres
(1780–1867), and in Italy where he studied the art of the Renaissance.

This portrait depicts the daughter of the industrialist and
collector, Henri Rouart. Degas painted Hélène throughout her life,
from childhood portraits on her father's knee to this thoughtful,
self-possessed pose in her father's study surrounded by objects from
his extensive art collection. Degas had a strong interest in the human
figure and continued working on this portrait in his studio until his
death in 1917, reworking the colours and adding stronger outlines.
This was typical of his 'passion for perfection' from preparatory
drawings in charcoal on paper, to thorough sketching on the canvas
before applying the paint layer. He had, as the art dealer Ambroise
Vollard (1866–1939) noted, a 'mania for adding final touches to his
pictures, no matter how finished they were'.

Private Worlds, Public Gaze

This section includes a particularly striking portrait by Degas of his sister (see cat 4). She stares directly at the viewer, with no attempt to dissemble or distract. It is interesting to compare our instinctive reaction when confronted with this penetrating gaze with that of seeing Walker Evans' photograph of *Allie Mae Burroughs*, 1936 (fig 2). The art historian Margaret Olin described this photograph as the product of the photographer's 'investment in the reality principle of documentary photography', explaining that 'when we look at the image we look at a woman. Just as important, the woman in the image appears to look at us…. a work of art, like a person, can seem to gaze or be gazed at. Within a work, gazes can be exchanged'.

It is the artist who controls the gaze, and manipulates the viewer's reaction. The works in this section embody the Impressionists' ability to capture life, including truly intimate moments, from quiet sewing to feeding an infant, and to transport this interior world onto a public stage.

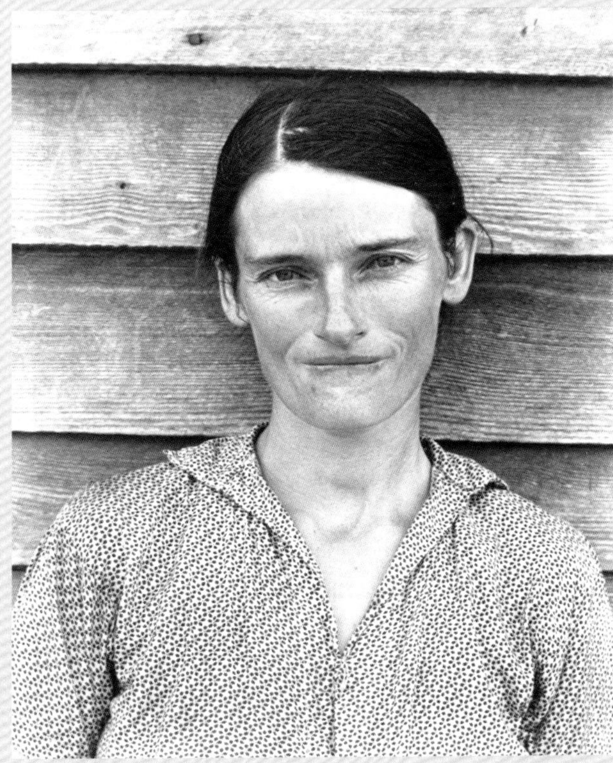

fig 2

Walker Evans (1903–1975)
Allie Mae Burroughs, Wife of a Cotton Sharecropper, Hale County, Alabama, 1936
Gelatin Silver print

Museum of Fine Arts, Houston, Texas, USA

cat 4

Edgar Degas (1834–1917)
Portrait de Marguerite, Soeur de l'artiste
(Portrait of Marguerite, the Artist's
Sister), c.1856
Oil on canvas
33.5 x 25.0 cm

The New Art Gallery Walsall
1973.033
Garman Ryan Collection

In his early twenties, Degas spent three years in Italy. The gravitas
of Italian Renaissance painting had a deep and lasting influence
on his style. This compelling portrait of his sister is direct and
uncompromising. Focusing more on line and form rather than the
effects of nature, Degas worked up compositions with rigorous
discipline based on numerous preparatory drawings and studies.
As a result his paintings demonstrate a solidity which sets him
apart from the practised spontaneity of his peers.

cat 5 (detail)

Camille Pissarro (1830–1903)
Petite bonne flamande dite 'La Rosa', 1896
Oil on canvas
54.6 x 45.1 cm

Richard Green Gallery, London

The subject clearly derives from Dutch and Flemish 17th-century
painting, perhaps inspired by the Flemish nationality of the sitter,
the artist's maidservant, Rosa. Pissarro went to Belgium in 1894 and
painted in Brussels. From the late 1880s, he became influenced by
the new 'pointillist' technique practiced by Georges Seurat, using dots
of colour to convey light. This is in evidence here, but in a softened
form, which characterised Pissarro's works from this moment
onwards. The painting was first exhibited at the Paris gallery of the
Impressionists' most instrumental supporter, Paul Durand-Ruel
(1831–1922), where it was praised as a 'superbly honest piece' and
'a delightful fragrance of rustic gracefulness'.

cat 6

Camille Pissarro (1830–1903)
Mme Pissarro Sewing Beside a Window,
1877
Oil on canvas
54.0 x 54.0 cm

The Ashmolean Museum, Oxford
WA1951.225.3
Pissarro Family Gift, 1951

Born in St. Thomas in the West Indies, Pissarro was educated in
Paris. The only artist to exhibit in all eight Impressionist exhibitions
between 1874 and 1886, he introduced Gauguin, Seurat and Signac
into the group. Pissarro originally trained with the Danish artist Fritz
Melbye (1826–1869) and, after moving to Paris in 1855, worked closely
with Jean-Baptiste-Camille-Corot (1796–1875) and Claude Monet. He
regularly used his own family as models. In this instance he combines
a subjective depiction of his industrious wife with an objective essay
in colour and form.

Of all the Impressionist artists, Pissarro was the most consistent.
This frank depiction of his daughter Jeanne-Rachel (also known
as Minette) conveys familiarity with the subject within a simple
interior with subdued light. The fan indicates the artist's interest
in Japanese art but appears somewhat awkwardly in his daughter's
hand, highlighting the contrived composition. The painting would
have gained poignancy for the artist after Jeanne's death from
tuberculosis the following year, aged nine.

cat 7

Camille Pissarro (1830–1903)
Jeanne Holding a Fan, 1873
Oil on canvas
56.0 x 46.5 cm

The Ashmolean Museum,
Oxford WA1952.6.2
Presented by the Pissarro
Family, 1952

Pierre-Auguste Renoir (1841–1919)
A Woman Nursing a Child, 1894
Oil on canvas
41.2 x 32.5 cm

Scottish National Gallery,
Edinburgh NG 2230
Presented by Sir Alexander
Maitland in memory
of his wife Rosalind, 1960

Renoir took part in the first four Impressionist exhibitions, but his success with wealthy patrons rendered him somewhat aloof from the group, and his work attracted the approval of the art establishment. Renoir's attitude towards women is hard to accept by today's standards. He famously noted 'I like women best when they don't know how to read'. Paradoxically his female portraits often convey an inherent respect for femininity. Here the calm mystery of motherhood is sympathetically observed. We feel privileged to be able to witness the mother and child in this intimate moment, the flush on the woman's cheek indicating her contentment. This simple painting becomes a quiet masterpiece translating the everyday into the exquisite.

Modern Life

fig 3

Edgar Degas (1834–1917)
L'Absinthe, 1873
Oil on canvas
92.0 x 68.5 cm

Musée d'Orsay
RF 1984

Edmond Renoir summarised his brother Pierre-Auguste's approach to naturalism:

'Does he make a portrait? He asks his model to maintain her customary manner, to sit as she usually sits, to dress the way she usually dresses, so that nothing smacks of constraint or artificial preparation. Thus his work has, in addition to its artistic value, all the "sui generis" charms of a painting faithful to modern life. What he has painted, we see before us everyday; he has recorded our lives in "pages" that will surely remain among the most vivid and harmonious of our period.'

Letter to Emile Bergerat, in *La Vie Moderne*, Paris, June 19, 1879

Despite this devotion to capturing realistic or truthful visions of the everyday, some of the most popular Impressionist figurative paintings invoke a glamorous, and often fictitious, world of leisure: figures reclining, couples wandering along the banks of the Seine, groups chatting at cafés, audience members spying on each other at the theatre. The world presented could be perceived as one simply of luxury and frivolity, where fashionable dress and places are captured with swirls of loosely applied paint. When the Impressionists seemingly broke from this mode, by depicting the rougher edge of society, public dissent quickly followed. *L'Absinthe* by Edgar Degas divided public opinion (see fig 3). Degas depicts two bohemians in the Nouvelle Athènes café, often frequented by Edouard Manet (1832–1883) and Degas. They are drinking alcohol at what, due to the presence of the morning papers, appears to be breakfast time. It is a gritty work, which conveys an infectious torpor and encourages the viewer to look twice to unravel the layers of meaning.

cat 9

Pierre-Auguste Renoir (1841–1919)
Young Woman Seated, 1876
Oil on canvas
66.0 x 55.0 cm

The Henry Barber Trust,
The Barber Institute of Fine Arts,
University of Birmingham
No 84.1

Nini Lopez was one of Renoir's preferred models. This work,
with delicate pastel tones, evokes the 18th-century French Rococo
period. Exhibited at the 1876 and 1877 Impressionist exhibitions,
it is typical of his most popular style denoting generic beauty
rather than specific portraits. This painting was known as
'La Pensée' (thought). The pose insinuates thoughts of a more
sensual than intellectual nature, indicated by the seductive
placement of the sitter's finger in her mouth, the frothy fabric
of her dress and her alluring gaze. Contrary to his brother's
beliefs (p.23), Renoir did not necessarily capture the 'everyday',
but instead painted fanciful works that he knew would appeal
to the predominantly male market.

The daughter of a high-ranking civil servant, Morisot was first
taught to draw by her father before undergoing formal instruction
under Joseph Guichard (1806–1880), a pupil of Jean-Baptiste-Camille
Corot (1796–1875). Having previously found success at the Salon, she
exhibited with the Impressionists from the first exhibition onwards.
She became a central figure, entertaining the group at her house on
a weekly basis. She married the brother of Edouard Manet in 1874 and
their daughter married the grandson of Degas' friend Henri Rouart
(see cat 3). This depiction of a model makes an interesting comparison
with Renoir's *Young Woman Seated* (cat 9). Where Renoir explored the
sensuality of his sitter, Morisot's depiction is more passive, with
a restrained palette and an even use of penetrating light. Morisot's
model leans back, self-assured, her attention caught elsewhere.
The result is every bit as captivating as Renoir's sexually-charged
depiction, and perhaps explores the theme of 'thought' with
increased complexity.

cat 10

Berthe Morisot (1841–1895)
Girl on a Divan, c.1885
Oil on canvas
61.0 x 50.2 cm

Tate T01079
Bequeathed by the Hon. Mrs A.E.
Pleydell-Bouverie through the
Friends of the Tate Gallery, 1968

Jean-Louis Forain (1852–1931)
Woman on a Chaise-longue, 1880s
Oil on panel
41.0 x 34.0 cm

The Ashmolean Museum,
Oxford WA1972.160
Bequeathed by Lt-Col
G.E. Bouskell-Wade, 1972

Forain regularly satirised the bourgeoisie and even in this depiction of a woman reclining we cannot be certain that the artist didn't intend to create a parody. The bold features and incisive lines, particularly marking out the eyebrows, eyes and nose, teeter on the verge of caricature. Highly influenced by Edouard Manet, Forain conveyed particular moods within his works with skilful artifice. Here we are aware that the sitter's languor has been interrupted by the artist. She has moved the fan away from her face and her left hand is poised ready to hoist her up out of the chaise and into action.

cat 12

Jean-Louis Forain (1852–1931)
The Fisherman, 1884
Oil on canvas
94.7 x 117.0 cm

Southampton City Art Gallery
204

Forain originally worked as a caricaturist, creating popular satirical illustrations for journals such as *La Vie Parisienne*. Forain's inclusion in four of the Impressionist exhibitions (1879, 1880, 1881, 1886) was divisive. Gustave Caillebotte (1848–1894), who had exhibited with the Impressionists since 1876 and made significant financial contributions to the group, deemed Forain, Jean-François Raffaelli (1850–1924) and Federico Zandomeneghi (1841–1917) to be inferior artists. This was in direct opposition to Degas who was a vociferous supporter of Forain's engaging style. *The Fisherman* typically blends humour – in the precarious positioning of the fisherman and his dog on the end of a jetty – with a subdued tone that gently evokes dusk.

cat 13

Georges Seurat (1859–1891)
Study for 'Une Baignade', c.1883
Oil on panel
15.9 x 25.0 cm

NG 2222
Scottish National Gallery, Edinburgh
Presented by Sir Alex Maitland in
memory of his wife Rosalind, 1960

Created three years before Seurat's first work in the 'pointillist' style that he initiated, this work has a distinctive fluidity of paint handling. Seurat's understanding of the effect of strong colours not only led to his famous technique of breaking up the surface into dots, but also led towards abstraction. Above all, Seurat excelled at capturing the essence of the world he inhabited. This small panel was one of many preparatory works for *The Bathers, Asnières* (National Gallery, London) based on studies of workers at rest by the Seine. It was rejected by the Salon in 1884. Painted 'en plein air' the panel that Seurat used here was the interior lid of his paint box, adding to the spontaneity and freshness of this delicate work.

cat 14

Eugène Boudin (1824–1898)
Road to Deauville, 1881
Oil on canvas
51.0 x 61.2 cm

Paisley Art Institute Collection held
at Paisley Museum & Art Galleries,
Renfrewshire Council A0155. From
the James Fulton Bequest, 1933

If Monet is sometimes called the father of Impressionism, the title
usurps the movement's true father, Boudin, who exhibited in the first
Impressionist exhibition of 1874 despite his relative seniority over his
young friends. An early practitioner of painting 'en plein air', Boudin
believed that painting three brushstrokes outdoors was far superior
to days spent labouring in the studio. He reflected: 'I may well have
had some small measure of influence on the movement that led
painters to study actual daylight and express the changing aspects
of the sky with the utmost sincerity.'

The beaches of Deauville and Trouville (in Normandy) were
immensely popular holiday locations for the fashionable elite
(Deauville inspired the coastal resort in Marcel Proust's *À la Recherche
du Temps Perdu*, 1909–22). Boudin and Monet collaborated on beach
scenes in Normandy in the 1860s, painting directly from nature.

Impressionism in Britain

The initial impact of Impressionism in Britain can be summed up by the reaction to one painting – *L'Absinthe* by Edgar Degas painted 1875–6 (fig 3). Shunned by critics after it was shown at Christie's in London in 1892, it was booed and hissed at by the public until taken off display. It was acquired by a Scottish dealer based in Glasgow, and subsequently bought by the collector Arthur Kay and exhibited again in London where it divided viewers. Some called it 'vulgar and immoral' others praised it as a 'literary performance'.

The more positive dissemination of French Impressionist ideals and approaches in Britain was largely due to the efforts of the art dealer Hugh Lane (1875–1915), the textile manufacturer Samuel Courtauld (1876–1947) and art collectors Gwendoline Davies (1882–1951) and Margaret Davies (1884–1963), the granddaughters of a wealthy industrialist. These four arbiters of taste consistently bought French paintings of the highest standard, which ultimately entered British public collections. In 1913 and 1918 important Impressionist exhibitions took place at the Victoria Art Gallery in Bath with major works lent by the Davies sisters. The physical movement of artists working in both France and England also created a cross-pollination of ideas, in particular through the works of James Abbott McNeill Whistler (1834–1903), Jacques Joseph Tissot (1836–1902) and Walter Richard Sickert (1860–1942).

In 1886 the New English Art Club was founded with fifty members. Set up as a rival to the Royal Academy (which had been established in 1768), it became the centre of modern British painting, particularly influenced by British artists who had trained in Paris such as Philip Wilson Steer and George Clausen. Lucien Pissarro, the eldest son of Camille, moved to England in 1890 and brought with him Post-Impressionist sensibilities. His striking portrait of his wife Esther Levi Bensusan was painted three years after he permanently settled in England (fig 4).

In a letter to his son, Camille Pissarro demonstrated awareness of his own perceived limited appeal to British sensibilities:

'…my works offend English taste. – Remember that I have the temperament of a peasant, I am melancholy, harsh and savage in my works, it is only in the long run that I can expect to please.'

Camille Pissarro to Lucien Pissarro, Rouen, 20 November 1883

In reality the impact of Impressionist works created a sea-change in Britain, leading to the creation of provocative schools of art from the New English Art Club to the Camden Town Group.

fig 4

Lucien Pissarro (1863–1944)
*Portrait of Esther in Profile
(portrait of the artist's wife)*, 1893
Oil on canvas
40.3 x 35.5 cm

Ferens Art Gallery, Hull City Council
KINCM:2005.5275

Alfred Sisley (1839–1899)
View of the Thames: Charing Cross,
1874
Oil on canvas
33.0 x 46.0 cm

Andrew Brownsword
Arts Foundation

This is Sisley's 'answer' to Monet's *Impression: Sunrise* (see p.8)
which had been included in the first Impressionist exhibition
in 1874. It was painted during a visit Sisley made to England
from July to October that year, in the company of his patron,
the singer Jean-Baptiste Faure. With exquisite delicacy, the
artist evokes the activity on the river as the dawn breaks
behind St. Paul's Cathedral.

cat 16

Philip Wilson Steer (1860–1942)
Girl on a Sofa, 1891
Oil on canvas
68.0 x 72.0 cm

Colchester and Ipswich
Museum Service
IPSMG: R:1987-98

Steer trained in Paris in 1882–3 where he assimilated the style in particular of Degas and Monet. He became a founding member of the New English Art Club and, with Walter Sickert, held an exhibition of 'London Impressionists' in December 1889.

This depiction of a girl reclining on a sofa with her left hand resting in a 'relaxed' pose, her head in profile and her eyes obscured by a curly fringe, demonstrates Steer's characteristic staged informality. It was hailed as one of Steer's greatest works when included in his one-man show at the Goupil Gallery in London in 1894. Often criticized for imitating the style of others, Steer was thought in this particular painting to have found his own voice. As the American author and art critic Elizabeth Robins Pennell (1855–1936) commented, with *Girl on a Sofa* Steer '…trusted entirely to his own way of looking at things in his own way of recording them. To…harmonious colour schemes and lovely decorative arrangement he brings a welcome freshness of treatment. Here he is wholly himself, not merely an echo of someone else'.

cat 17

Sir George Clausen (1852–1944)
Portrait of a Girl's Head, 1886
Oil on canvas
56.7 x 44.5 cm

Manchester Art Gallery
1922.4

fig 5

Jules Bastien-Lepage (1848–1884)
Going to School, 1882
Oil on canvas
80.9 x 59.8 cm

Aberdeen Art Gallery &
Museums Collection
ABDAG002288

George Clausen, like Steer, was a founding member of the New English Art Club. He was introduced to French art through a chance meeting in 1880 with Jules Bastien-Lepage who inspired him to move away from genre scenes influenced by the Dutch Old Masters and to embrace depictions of rural everyday life (see fig 5). In order to capture real-life scenes of labourers in the fields, Clausen sketched from life and made use of photography to aid his memory.

In the 1890s Clausen became influenced by the French Impressionists, in particular Degas, in his positioning of figures and varied viewpoints. His reputation and standing in British art circles was enhanced by his appointment as Professor of Painting at the Royal Academy Schools in 1903.

This direct portrait is typical of Clausen's approach, with a compelling angle of the sitter's head and slightly indirect gaze. The intense green of the leafy background echoes the sitter's eyes. The distinct patterns of the leaves in the right-hand background transform into simple rectangular blocks of paint on the left, adding dynamic tension to the simple composition.

In 1902 the Goupil Gallery staged Clausen's first one-man show which featured twenty oil paintings and thirty-one works on paper. His pastels proved particularly popular with the influential art critic and fellow New English Art Club member D S MacColl remarking 'The stroke of the pastel chalk seems to be the most direct and satisfactory means of expression for Mr Clausen'.

The artist's son, Hugh Clausen, an engineer who lived and worked in Bath, presented a number of his late father's works to the Holburne Museum in 1949. The following eight works were all part of this gift.

cat 18

Sir George Clausen (1852–1944)
Portrait Sketch of a Young Girl,
c.1892
Pastel on brown paper
23.8 x 17.5 cm

Holburne Museum A356.3
—

cat 19

Sir George Clausen (1852–1944)
Portrait Head of a Young Girl,
c.1895
Black chalk and pastel on
brown paper
36.3 x 22.5 cm

Holburne Museum A356.9
—

cat 20

Sir George Clausen (1852–1944)
Portrait sketch of a Young Woman,
c.1890
Black chalk on white paper
30.0 x 22.5 cm

Holburne Museum A356.48
—

cat 21

Sir George Clausen (1852–1944)
Study of a Young Girl, c.1895/6
Black chalk and pastel on paper
36.3 x 23.8 cm

Holburne Museum A356.44
—

cat 22

Sir George Clausen (1852–1944)
Study of a Female Nude, c.1918
Chalk and conté on paper
31.3 x 23.8 cm

Holburne Museum A356.23
—

cat 23

Sir George Clausen (1852–1944)
Study for The Boy and The Man, c.1905–7
Black chalk, pencil and watercolour
on paper
48.8 x 23.8 cm

Holburne Museum A356.34
—

cat 24

Sir George Clausen (1852–1944)
*Study of a Young Woman bearing
a Load on her Head*, c.1900
Black chalk and pastel on paper
38.8 x 27.5 cm

Holburne Museum A356.15
—

cat 25

Sir George Clausen (1852–1944)
Study of a Harvester, c.1890
Black chalk and pastel on paper
38.8 x 27.5 cm

Holburne Museum A356.45
—

cat 26

Walter Richard Sickert (1860–1942)
The Lady in the Gondola, 1905
Oil on canvas
30.0 x 35.0 cm

The Ashmolean Museum, Oxford
WA 1940.1.17
Hindley Smith Bequest, 1939

Like Steer (cat 16) Sickert assimilated different elements of Impressionism and his style changed frequently throughout his life. Sickert lived in Dieppe between 1899 and 1905, spending his winters in Venice. He settled near Bath for the last four years of his life. Sickert was particularly influenced by Degas in his use of unusual angles and distinct viewpoints. Here, he captures Mrs George Swinton mid-expression, her head thrown backwards as though she is about to speak or laugh. The deliberately awkward positioning places the artist (and the viewer) in the gondola looking upwards towards the sitter. With a sense of fleeting immediacy, the movement of her head is starkly contrasted with the permanency of the elegant church of Il Redentore behind.

cat 27

Walter Richard Sickert (1860–1942)
The Bust of Tom Sayers: a Self-Portrait,
c.1913–15
Oil on canvas
61.0 x 50.3 cm

The Ashmolean Museum,
Oxford WA 2001.35. Presented by the
Christopher Sands Trust, 2001

Curiously, Sickert included the bust of the boxer Tom Sayers (1826–1865) in many of the paintings and drawings that he created during the First World War. With dark intensity, the composition pits the artist against the fighter, balanced by an elegant blue and white vase. A Camden Town local hero, Sayers had been the heavyweight champion of England in the mid-19th century despite his comparatively slight build. The painting therefore acts as a defiant challenge with the bearded artist presenting himself as a brooding force to be reckoned with.

cat 28

Sir John Lavery (1856–1901)
Paisley Lawn Tennis Club, 1889
Oil on canvas
71.0 cm x 81.0 cm

Paisley Art Institute Collection held
at Paisley Museum & Art Galleries,
Renfrewshire Council A0102.
Presented by James Begg, 1917

Lavery was born in Northern Ireland and moved to Glasgow in the
1870s to study at the Haldane Academy and he later trained at the
Académie Julian in Paris. Like Clausen, Lavery was heavily influenced
by Bastien-Lepage (see fig 5). As a member of the internationally-
renowned Glasgow Boys, he was inspired by the French
Impressionists and became a champion for the works of Whistler.

   Lawn tennis was first played in Britain in 1865 and soon
became a popular leisure pastime for Lavery's circle of wealthy
patrons. Here he depicts a match between Miss Nina Fullerton and a
male companion at the Lawn Tennis Club at Paisley (which still exists
today). The view of the game is obscured by the spectacular blossom
of a cherry tree, under which the spectators seek shade and converse.
The influence of Impressionism and naturalism is evident in Lavery's
seemingly effortless evocation of the informal scene. He conveys
the action while simultaneously creating a highly decorative tableau
in which the spectators, the players and the dappled light are all
subject to our captivated gaze.

Further Reading

Bruce Bernard (ed.), *The Impressionist Revolution,* London, 1986

Robert L Herbert, *Impressionism: Art, Leisure and Parisian Society,* New Haven and London, 1991

Michael Howard (ed.), *The Impressionists by Themselves,* London, 1998

Martha Kapos (ed.), *The Impressionists: A Retrospective,* New York, 1991

Madeleine Korn, 'Exhibitions of Modern French Art and their Influence on Collectors in Britain 1870–1918: The Davies Sisters in Context', *Journal of the History of Collections,* Vol. 16, No. 2, 2004, pp. 191–218

Melissa McQuillan, *Impressionist Portraits,* London, 1986

Sylvie Patry (ed.), *Inventing Impressionism: Paul Durand-Ruel and the Modern Art Market,* London, 2015

John Rewald, *The History of Impressionism,* New York, 1961

James H Rubin, *Impressionism,* London, 1999

Meyer Schapiro, *Impressionism: Reflections and Perceptions,* New York, 1997

Basil Taylor, *The Impressionists and their World,* London, 1953

Paul Hayes Tucker, 'The First Impressionist Exhibition and Monet's *Impression, Sunrise*: A Tale of Timing, Commerce and Patriotism', *Art History,* Vol. 7, No. 4, December 1984, pp. 465–76

Image Credits

Catalogue illustrations

1, 10 — © Tate, London 2016

2 — © CSG CIC Glasgow Museums and Libraries Collections

3 — © The National Gallery, London

4 — The New Art Gallery Walsall

5 — Richard Green Gallery, London

6, 7, 11, 26, 27 — © Ashmolean Museum, University of Oxford

8, 13 — Scottish National Gallery, Edinburgh

9 — The Barber Institute of Fine Arts, University of Birmingham

12 — © Southampton City Art Gallery / Bridgeman Images

14, 28 — Paisley Art Institute Collection held at Paisley Museum & Art Galleries, Renfrewshire Council

15 — Photo © The National Gallery, London. On loan from the Andrew Brownsword Arts Foundation

16 — Colchester and Ipswich Museum Service

17 — © Manchester Art Gallery / Bridgeman Images

18 to 25 — © The Holburne Museum. Photography by Dan Brown

Figure illustrations

fig 1 — © The National Gallery, London

fig 2 — © Museum of Fine Arts, Houston, Texas, USA / Bridgeman Images

fig 3 — © RMN-Grand Palais (Musée d'Orsay) / Martine Beck-Coppola

fig 4 — Ferens Art Gallery, Hull Museums, UK / Photo © Christie's Images / Bridgeman Images

fig 5 — Aberdeen Art Gallery & Museums Collection

Every effort has been made to secure all necessary permissions to reproduce images within this book. Any errors or omissions should be addressed to the Holburne Museum.

Published to accompany the exhibition

Impressionism: *Capturing Life*

The Holburne Museum
13 February to 5 June 2016

The Holburne Museum
Great Pulteney Street
Bath BA2 4DB
www.holburne.org
Registered charity no. 310288

Published by The Holburne Museum
ISBN 978-0-903679-06-0
Book © The Holburne Museum, 2016
Text © Jennifer Scott, 2016
Design: Northbank, Bath

In Partnership with Bath Spa University

Back cover:
cat 1 (detail)

John Singer Sargent (1856–1925)
*Claude Monet Painting by
the Edge of a Wood,* 1885